110

# TRAINS AT WORK

# TRAINS
## AT WORK

*By Mary Elting*

ILLUSTRATED BY
### DAVID LYLE MILLARD

HARVEY HOUSE, INC.
Irvington-on-Hudson, N. Y.

## SAM IS AN ENGINEER

Sam is the engineer on a freight locomotive. Like many people who work on trains, Sam belongs to a family of railroaders. His father was the engineer on a big steam locomotive. His grandfather was a fireman. And long ago, his great-grandmother was an "op." That means she operated the telegraph in a railroad station. The messages she sent helped to keep the trains running safely and on time.

When Sam was a little boy, he listened to his father and grandfather talking railroad talk. They used all kinds of words that ordinary people didn't understand. They had wonderful nicknames for each other and slang words for many of the things they did.

For instance, Sam's father called his big locomotive a hog. Since he ran it, he was the hogger. After every trip, he brought his engine to the roundhouse, where men cleaned it and fixed it up. Pig-pen was one nickname for the roundhouse. You can easily see why. Another nickname was barn, because people often called a locomotive an Iron Horse. The barn had stalls for engines like the ones in the picture on the next page. The engines burned coal, and the roundhouse was a smoky place when several locomotives were getting up steam or having their ashes taken out.

Sam's engine is a Diesel. It uses oil, which burns without making clouds of smoke. Diesels need much less care than coal-burning locomotives, and so roundhouses aren't really necessary. But some railroads that have roundhouses still use them as Diesel repair shops.

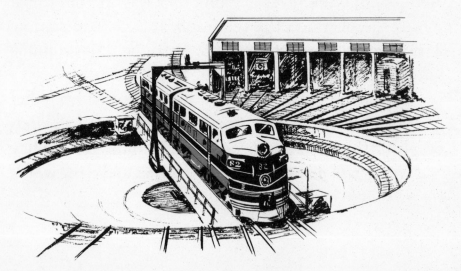

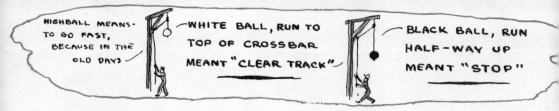

In the old days the fireman shoveled coal into the engine's fire box. That was his main job. He said the lumps of coal were black diamonds, and he called his shovel his banjo. The other men called him diamond pusher or bakehead or ashcat.

An old-fashioned train was hard to stop after it began rolling. A man had to run from car to car, putting on the brakes by hand. Naturally, he was the brakeman, but his friends called him the shack.

Before electric lights were invented, railroaders needed signals, just as they do now. The first ones were large balls that hung from a tall post. A black ball hanging halfway to the top meant STOP. A white ball hanging high in the air meant CLEAR TRACK.

Many things have changed since then, but a signal to go ahead is still the "highball." Railroaders like to use the old words. Machinery now sets the train's brakes, but one of the crew is still called a brakeman. There is no fire to tend on a Diesel locomotive, but the engineer's helper is almost always called the fireman.

When Sam reports for work, his locomotive is ready. Men have carefully inspected it. The whole long train of

freight cars behind it has been inspected, too. Sam and
the fireman and the brakeman climb aboard. They work
at the front of the train, so they are called the head-end-
crew. Another brakeman and the freight conductor
work in the caboose — the last car on the train. In between the caboose and the engine are
nearly a hundred cars of freight that
must be delivered fast. A fast freight is
called a hotshot or redball. A slow one is
a drag.

Sam moves the throttle lever, and
the long train pulls out of the freight
yard onto the main line. Sam sits on the
right side of the cab and watches the
track ahead. The fireman sits on the left.
He keeps a sharp lookout, too. When

they come to a curve, he looks back along the train to make sure everything is all right.

After a while they see a little town up ahead, and beside the track stands a signal they have been expecting. It looks like a round plate, with places for nine lights in it. But only three of the lights are ever flashed at once. Other railroads have other types of signals, but the lights always mean the same: green for go ahead, yellow for go slowly, and red for stop.

This time the go-ahead lights are showing.

"Clear signal," the fireman calls out.

"Green eye it is," Sam replies.

All through the trip the two men will call the signals back and forth to each other, just to make sure there is no mistake. For extra safety, some locomotives also have small automatic signal lights inside the cab.

Sam gives one long blast on his horn to tell the station agent in the little town that the train is coming. As they pass the station, the fireman leans out of the cab and snatches something from the agent's hand.

Railroaders say that the fireman has been "catching

a butterfly." What he took from the station agent really does look like a butterfly. It is a piece of paper tied around the middle and fastened to a metal hoop.

The fireman takes the paper off and quickly tosses the hoop out of the cab. In the meantime the agent hands another hoop to the conductor in the caboose.

The paper is a train order, called a flimsy. On the flimsy the station agent has written instructions for the train's crew. Orders come to his station by telephone or telegraph. Sometimes they tell the crew that the train must make an unexpected stop before the next station. Sometimes they give information about other trains that have been delayed.

The station agent has to follow very strict rules when he writes out the train orders. For instance, he must not erase anything, because that might make a fuzzy spot, and a fuzzy order might cause an accident. After the train goes by, the agent walks along the track and picks up the hoops. One agent trained his dog to chase the hoops and bring them back!

Sam and the fireman and the brakeman all read the orders. If by any chance Sam should forget to do what the orders tell him to do, the others are supposed to remind him.

Some railroads send orders by teletype, which is a

combination telegraph and typewriter. A man in the main office typewrites the orders on his machine. It is connected with another machine in the station agent's office. Automatically the agent's machine types out just what the man in the main office wrote.

Many railroads have radio telephones. There is one phone in the locomotive and another in the caboose. The main office can talk to both the engineer and the conductor and give them orders.

The conductor on Sam's train reads his copy of the flimsy, then goes back to his desk. The caboose is his office. There he checks the papers that tell what is in every freight car and where it is going.

The brakeman drinks a cup of the coffee that he has

been heating on the stove in the caboose. Then he climbs to his seat in the cupola — the little tower with windows through which he can watch the train. Squirrel cage is a nickname for the cupola. The caboose has the most nicknames of all. Crib, crummy, crum box, bounce, doghouse, parlor, and monkey house are some of them.

Safety is everybody's job on a train, and each man has certain things that he is supposed to do. If the train makes an emergency stop, the two brakemen must make sure that no other train bumps into them. One brakeman runs out ahead and the other runs back along the track with signals to warn other trains. They set out red flags in the daytime, and red lamps at night. Day and night they light fusees, which look like giant firecrackers and burn with a bright red glow.

In addition, the brakeman lays torpedoes on the track and fastens them with little clamps. If a locomotive runs over the torpedoes, they explode with loud bangs that tell the engineer to stop before he runs into the stalled train ahead.

The first regular stop for Sam's train is a station where he pulls his train off onto a side track and waits for a fast passenger train to go by.

On the next part of Sam's trip, the train has to climb some steep grades. In the old days, one steam locomotive

alone couldn't pull a long train up the mountain, so a helper engine coupled on, in the middle or just ahead of the caboose. If the train was extra long and heavy, two helpers were needed, and each had its own crew.

When Sam's Diesel engine needs help, extra sections couple on at the head end, and they don't need any extra men to take care of them. If something goes wrong in any of the Diesels, a warning bell rings. Maybe a fuse has blown out or a wire has come loose. It is the fireman's job to hunt for the trouble and fix it.

Going downhill in the mountains is work, too — work for the brakes. On old-fashioned trains, the brakeman had to run along the tops of freight cars and "club down." That means he used a long club, called a sap, to turn the wheels that set the hand brakes on each car.

The catwalks or decks along the car roofs made a path for the brakemen. Sometimes they walked up and down the decks inspecting the train. Then they said they were "deckorating."

Cars now have air brakes which are worked by compressed air. An air hose is connected to brake machinery under every car. The hose on each car can be joined to the hoses on the cars next to it, and the front car's hose connects with the locomotive. A pump in the locomotive makes compressed air for the whole train.

Air brakes are built for safety. This is how they work: air pressure pushes the brakes away from the wheels. If the engineer wants to stop the train, he moves a lever. Air goes out of the hoses, and the brakes squeeze tight against the wheels. This same thing happens if a hose accidentally begins to leak. Air goes out; the brakes automatically squeeze the wheels; the train stops, and the brakeman knows he must look for the hole.

An engineer must learn how to use the brakes so that the cars don't jerk as they lose speed. If he does the job well, the whole train will slow down smoothly.

When a train goes down a very long hill, the squeezing of the brakes can actually make the wheels get red hot. This happens less now than it used to, because the machinery in a Diesel locomotive can act as a brake that helps to hold the train back on a hill.

STOP
SWING BACK
AND FORTH
ACROSS TRACKS

REDUCE SPEED
HELD AT
ARM'S LENGTH
HORIZONTALLY

PROCEED
RAISED AND
LOWERED
VERTICALLY

After a while Sam's train runs into a storm in the cold, high mountains. Slushy snow has frozen on the rails. Instead of pulling ahead, the engine's wheels begin to slip around and around.

But Sam can fix this easily. He squirts some sand onto the slick track to make the wheels pull again. The sand drops down from a box through pipes onto the tracks just in front of the engine's wheels.

Rain and even the dampness in a tunnel can make the tracks almost as slippery as ice. So a locomotive's sand is just as important as its fuel. Railroads keep supplies of it on hand. When a locomotive stops to take on oil, its sand box is checked and filled at the same time.

At last Sam pulls into a big freight yard, and his part of the run is finished. After a while he will board another engine and take another freight train back to his home station. He has a regular schedule for work. That doesn't seem strange to us, but Sam's railroading ancestors would have thought it was miraculous.

In the old days, an engineer never knew what time he'd have to leave for work. Sometimes, when he was ready to blow out the kerosene lamp and go to bed,

there would be a loud knock at the door. On the dark porch he'd see a boy, still panting from a bicycle ride up the street. This was the railroad call boy, and he had come to say that an engineer was needed right away. No matter how sleepy the engineer was, he had to pull on his clothes and report for work.

But a train with a tired crew isn't safe. Now there are rules that say how long a trip the engineer can make in one day. Sam ends his trip at a place called a division point. Other men will speed the train along the next division of its run.

## UNSCRAMBLING THE TRAINS

Sam's engine brought almost a hundred freight cars over the mountains. Now the cars have to be separated. Some of them are going to Baltimore. Some will go to Chicago. Others must be delivered in New Orleans.

Freight cars for twenty different cities are coupled together in one train, and somebody must unscramble
them. What is the easiest way to do the job?

You can see how it is done if you imagine that you
have a lot of colored beads on a string. You want to
separate them into greens and reds and blues. The easiest
way is to get three cups and let the beads drop off one
by one, each into its own cup with the others of the
same color.

That's just what railroaders do with a freight train.
Instead of cups, of course, they have many separate
tracks, all branching off a main track. On one branch
track, they collect the cars that go to Baltimore; on an-

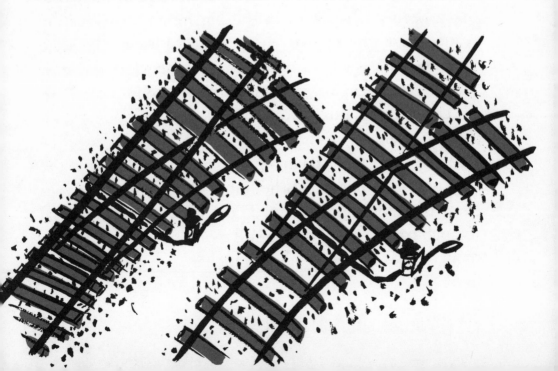

other, the cars for Chicago; on others, the cars headed for still different cities. This system of tracks is a classification yard.

In order to turn the cars from one track to another, there must be switches. A switch is made of movable pieces of rail that guide the cars' wheels. Look back at the picture on page 25, and you will see how a switch guides a car either along the main track or onto a branch track that curves to the right.

Some of the most wonderful inventions in the world have been put to work in the big freight classification yards. First, the regular engine usually leaves the train and a special switch engine couples on. The engineer of the switch engine has a radio telephone in the cab, so he can listen to orders from the towerman who unscrambles the train.

The towerman sits in a tower beside the track at the top of a little hill called the hump. The main track goes over the hump and down. Then it divides into several branch tracks which divide still more. In a big yard there may be two dozen or more branches.

LOOKING OUT OF INSPECTOR'S
PIT AT CAR PASSING OVERHEAD

When a car is uncoupled just at the top of the hump, it will roll down the slope by itself. To make the car go onto the proper branch, the towerman works an electric switch. He simply pushes small handles on the board in front of him, and electric machinery moves the switches in the tracks.

On the desk beside him, the towerman has a list that tells him where each car in the train is and what city it is headed for. He knows which branch tracks should be used — for example, track number 4 for cars going to Baltimore, track 6 for Chicago cars.

Slowly the switch engine pushes the train toward the hump. On the way the cars pass over a big hole underneath the track. In the hole sits a man in a chair that can be tipped and turned. And all around are bright lights that shine on the undersides of cars as they pass. This is the inspection pit. The man in the chair tilts this way and that, watching through a shatterproof glass hood to see if anything is broken or loose. When he spots a car that needs repairing, he talks with the towerman by radio

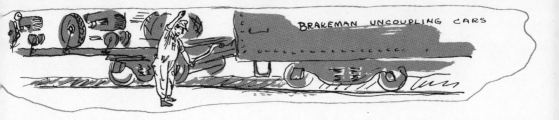
BRAKEMAN UNCOUPLING CARS

telephone. The towerman switches the car off onto a repair track.

In some yards the inspector pushes a button that makes whitewash squirt onto a car to mark it for repair. In other yards, inspection is done with a TV camera that shows close-up pictures of the cars as they pass by.

When the first car reaches the hump, a brakeman uncouples it. Slowly it starts downhill. Then it gathers speed. If it hits another car, there will be a crash. But, like magic, something seems to grab the wheels and slow them down. Something does reach out from the sides of the track. It is the car retarder. It squeezes against the wheels and keeps them from rolling too fast.

The retarder works by electricity. A thinking ma-

LOOKING DOWN INTO PIT AT THE
INSPECTOR AND HIS SEARCHLIGHTS—

chine operates it. Before the car goes over the hump, the thinking machine is given a lot of information — how much the car weighs, whether the wind will hold it back, how easily its wheels are rolling. The thinking machine then puts all these facts together and sends the car retarder a message that makes it press just hard enough against the wheels to slow this particular car. Another retarder farther along slows it still more.

Before railroads had this machinery, brakemen went over the hump with the cars, working fast and hard to put the hand brakes on at just the right time. Brakemen who did this were called hump riders.

Car after car drifts down the hump and stops just where it should. When one freight train has been un-

scrambled, another rolls up beneath the tower. Its cars, too, are shuffled and added to the new trains.

In some yards a man stands beside the track that leads to the hump. He holds something that looks like a gun. It is — an oil gun. As the cars pass, he takes aim and fires a stream of oil straight into boxes on the wheels. In some yards the gun fires automatically with the help of a magic eye — the kind that opens supermarket doors. It saves time to oil the wheels before the cars are switched.

There are several kinds of switch engine built especially for their jobs. In the old days switching was often done with a worn-out engine. Railroad men called an old wheezy engine a teakettle. An ordinary

Diesel Switcher

electric switcher

"teakettle"

**back in**

**hot box**

**train should back away**

**come in on track four**

switch engine is called a bobtail or a yard goat.

Very small railroad yards don't have switches that work by electricity. So switchmen work them by hand. A switchman used to be called a cherry picker, because of the red lights on the switches. Another nickname for him was snake. That's because he used to wear a union button with a big snaky S on it. Most railroaders belong to unions called Brotherhoods. Part of the safety of their work was brought about by the unions which helped to get laws passed and rules established to make railroading as free from danger as possible.

In the old days, one great danger came from the big, heavy gadget called a link-and-pin that joined the cars together. The switchman or the brakeman had to reach in and fasten it when a train was being made up. If the cars began to move while he was at work, he got his fingers cut off.

All cars now have automatic cou-

32

plings which clasp together and hold tight when one car bumps another. To uncouple, the switchman works a handle that keeps his fingers safely out of the way.

A railroad yard is a noisy place. Usually the engineer can't possibly talk with a switchman down the track, no matter how loud he shouts. In many yards the two men use radio telephones. Long before radios were invented, railroaders worked out a whole sign language in which they could send messages from a distance. The pictures tell what some of these special signs mean.

After a new freight train has been made up at the classification yard, a car inspector puts a blue flag on the engine and another on the caboose. Then he checks up carefully on the whole train to make sure everything is in good working order. An old nickname for inspector was car toad, because he often squatted down to look for broken parts. While he is at work, the blue flags

cut off car or engine

bad order car

couple cars

time to eat

TRAIN PARTED — SWING VERTICALLY IN CIRCLE AT ARM'S LENGTH ACROSS TRACKS

APPLY AIR BRAKES — SWUNG HORIZONTALLY ABOVE HEAD

RELEASE AIR BRAKES — HELD AT ARM'S LENGTH ABOVE THE HEAD.

are a warning that the train must not be disturbed. If the inspector finds a car that needs repairs, he reports that it is a bad-order car. If it cannot be fixed on the spot, it goes to a repair track called the rip track.

All kinds of new things are being invented to make work easier and safer in the freight classification yards. A new signal lamp gets its light from a tiny atomic power plant inside. It guards switches in freight yards, and it is supposed to burn for ten years, night and day. A small electric feeler on the track can discover cracked wheels long before an inspector's eyes can detect them.

But there are still many jobs that only people can do. Nobody has yet invented a machine that can uncouple the cars. Men have to open the boxes on car wheels before the automatic gun can squirt oil in. And no thinking machine could take the place of the head-end crew.

RAILROAD SHOPS

Locomotives and cars have regular inspections, and small repair jobs are done in the yards. But after a while they begin to wear out, and then they go to the shops for overhauling.

A locomotive shop has rails on the floor and rails in the air, too. A locomotive rolls in on its own tracks

34

and stops beside a platform. An
overhead crane also travels on
rails high above the floor. The crane swoops down, picks
the Diesel engine out of the locomotive, and carries it off.

35

A Diesel doesn't have to wait for repair men to fix its insides. In a little while the crane comes back with a spare engine to replace the one it took out.

Locomotives and cars have their wheels tested in the shops. Wheel experts used to have a special way of telling a good one from a cracked one. They gave it a sharp rap with a hammer. If the metal rang out clear and bell-like, it was supposed to be all right. Inspectors in the yards went about tapping car wheels, too. That's how repairmen and inspectors got their nicknames — car knocker, car-whacker, car-tinker, car-tink, car-tonk.

Shop men now have scientific tests for wheels and axles. Sometimes they take X-rays that show cracks hidden deep in the metal. Sometimes they use a device called an echoscope which tests metal with a special kind of sound wave. It can tell by the echo of the sound whether there are any weak spots.

Nothing in a railroad shop goes to waste. When big metal parts are shaved and smoothed, even the shavings are kept. A machine with a magnet inside sorts the tiny bits of metal. The iron bits stick to the magnet, and other kinds drop through into containers. Later each kind is melted to make new parts. Iron dust from a locomotive's axle may turn up later in one of the thousands of new car wheels that railroads keep on hand in huge yards.

37

## LOCOMOTIVES

When your father was your age, most locomotives burned coal. The coal fire under the boiler heated water to make steam. The steam turned the locomotive's huge driving wheels. Used-up steam left the engine in noisy puffs, and the sound had a regular rhythm — choo-choo, choo-choo.

Steam also made the locomotive's whistle blow. Using short toots and long ones, the engineer could send messages in railroad language to the crew and to anyone along the tracks.

A Diesel locomotive's wheels are not turned by steam, and so it doesn't have a steam whistle. It has a horn (sometimes two horns) instead. Everyone loved the sad, lonesome sound of steam whistles, and when railroads began to use Diesels, people complained about the ugly sound of the horns. In fact, there was such a fuss about the horns that railroads tried to make them imitate the old-fashioned whistles. But it was no use. People could tell the difference.

There used to be more than forty different kinds of steam locomotive at work on railroads. The only ones left are a few that run once or twice a year just to entertain people who still love them. Some railroads use electric locomotives. The wheels of these engines are turned by electric motors that get their current from wires along the tracks.

Diesel locomotives are really Diesel-electrics. They have oil-burning engines that turn electric generators right in the locomotive. Current from the generators runs electric motors that turn the wheels.

A Diesel cannot pull a heavy load as fast as one of the old steam locomotives could, but a Diesel can start

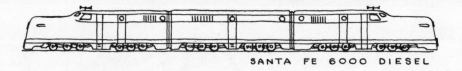

SANTA FE 6000 DIESEL

faster and it can start more smoothly. It doesn't need to stop so often to take on fuel, and it never needs to take on huge quantities of water for the boiler. It never has ashes to clean out.

The cab of a coal-burning locomotive had to be built between the coal car and the fire box. This meant that the engineer and the fireman didn't always have a very clear view of the track ahead. They often kept the windows open so they could see better. A Diesel's cab is at the very front, and the men can see far ahead. Besides, there is no smoke or steam to hide the view.

Diesel locomotives are built in sections called units. The A-unit is the one with the cab. It can pull a train all by itself. The B-units have no cabs. They are helpers that

SANTA FE DIESEL-ELECTRIC ROAD SWITCHING ENGINES

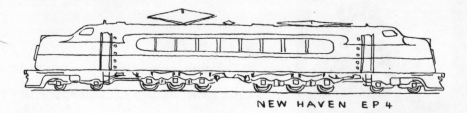

NEW HAVEN EP 4

are added to an A-unit when a train is very long and heavy or when it has to climb up over mountains. Big Diesel switching engines often have several units, too.

A few gas-turbine locomotives are at work hauling fast freight trains. They burn oil, which turns into hot gases. As the hot gases leave the engine, they make a sort of fan, called a turbine, whirl around and around. The turbine whirls an electric generator, and electricity then makes the locomotive's wheels turn.

Inventors have also made a new kind of engine called a Diesel-hydraulic. Instead of turning wheels by electricity, it works something like an automobile or a truck that has an automatic gear shift.

Some day there may be locomotives that are run by atomic energy.

GAS-TURBINE LOCOMOTIVE

## HOT BOXES

Have you ever been on a train that stopped suddenly between stations? Perhaps one of the cars had a hot box. That is railroaders' way of saying that one of the axles needs more oil.

Car axles must be kept well oiled in order to turn smoothly. They are fixed so that each end of the axle turns on an oily pad that is very much like a plastic foam pillow with a shaggy pillowcase. The pad is about as wide and as long as this book and five inches thick. The container that holds this pad is the journal box, and there's one for each wheel.

Inspectors always check journal boxes carefully, but it sometimes happens that the oil in the pad gets used up while the car is moving. The unoiled axle grows hotter and hotter, and the pad begins to smoke. The car has a hot box, which railroaders also call a stinker. Hot boxes can be dangerous. If an axle turns too long without oil, it may break off and cause an accident.

When the train goes around a curve, the engineer or the fireman looks back to see if there are any smoking journal boxes. The brakeman and the conductor in the caboose watch, too. The conductor can call by radio telephone and tell the engineer to stop for a stinker. If necessary, the conductor can put on the emergency air brake, and that stops the whole train fast.

Although a hot box is dangerous, it's easy to remedy. The box only needs a new pad or more oil on the old pad.

Everybody who works on a railroad watches for hot boxes. When workers take a good look at a moving train, they say they have made a running inspection. Some railroads have automatic detectors for hot boxes. One kind sits on the ground beside the track. It is very sensitive to heat. If a car with a hot box goes past it, the detector sends a message to a signal box ahead. When the train comes to the signal, the engineer sees it and stops. Another detector sends signals to a thinking machine. The machine changes the signals into words, which go by radio telephone to tell the engineer exactly which car has the hot box!

The newest, fastest cars on both passenger and

freight trains get fewer hot boxes than old ones. Their axles have roller bearings to help them turn smoothly, and the oil in their journal boxes is supposed to last for a long time. Still, an inspector may forget to check the oil, or it may leak out.

There's no padding around roller bearings. So how is anyone going to tell when one of the new cars gets a hot box? Some railroads have solved the problem with bombs! Into every journal box go two little gadgets that explode when an unoiled axle begins to heat up. One bomb lets out a big puff of smoke that can easily be seen. The other spills a nasty smelling gas that is sure to make passengers complain, in case the conductor doesn't notice it himself.

GREENBALL FREIGHT

Roller-bearings are usually put on the freight cars that need to run at passenger train speed. Greenball

44

freight always travels fast. A greenball train carries fruits and vegetables in refrigerator cars, which are also called reefers or riffs.

Some reefers have cooling machinery that can make the car very cold. They carry frozen food, which must not be allowed to thaw out while it is travelling.

The reefers that carry ordinary fresh food are cooled with ice. They have large containers called bunkers at both ends, and at most stations men put ice into the bunkers by hand. But a big loading station has a giant icing machine to do the job. It rides along on its own rails, poking its great arms out and pouring tons of ice into the cars.

When fruit and vegetables are loaded in hot weather, the reefer may need extra cooling. Onto the loading platform rolls a machine with a big canvas funnel that fits tightly over the reefer's door. This is a blower that forces cold air into the car. Now the crates or baskets of food can be loaded quickly, and the door is sealed shut. Fans keep cool air moving around and around inside the car while it is travelling to market.

When fruit trains from California go across the high mountains in winter, there is danger that the reefers may get too cold. So little charcoal stoves are put into the bunkers for the mountain trip. The bunkers are filled with ice again when they get to warmer country.

Bananas and some other fruits have to be inspected on the road to make sure they are not spoiling. The inspectors are called messengers.

Reefers also carry meat and fish, butter, eggs and cheese. Whole carloads of all these fresh foods roll into big towns and cities where they can be used up quickly before they spoil. But there are many small towns where people don't need a whole reefer full of butter or fish. For these places some railroads have built special refrigerator boxes. Three of the boxes fit onto a flat car. As the train moves across the country, the boxes can be taken off one by one at small freight stations. Other trains will pick up the boxes when they are empty.

## TO MARKET, TO MARKET

These two black sheep are railroad workers riding to work in Texas. They really do have jobs at stock pens, helping the men load other sheep into the livestock cars that carry them to market. If you have ever tried to drive sheep along, you know that they get confused and contrary. They will scatter in every direction except the right one. But, if they have a leader to show them the way, they will follow quietly behind him.

So railroaders and stockyard workers often teach certain sheep to lead others up the ramp and into the stock car. When the last one is in, the lead sheep runs out, and the door slams shut. Black sheep are best for the job because they stand out from the usual white ones, and they don't get sent off to market by mistake.

Perhaps you wonder how it is possible to teach sheep to do this kind of job. The answer is that they get a treat every time they finish loading a car. Some pets like sugar or a carrot, but these two were fondest of a big piece of chewing tobacco.

Stock cars for sheep and pigs have two decks. Cars for cattle and horses and mules have only one. And poultry cars have several. The slits in livestock cars let in plenty of fresh air and keep the animals cool. Since pigs are likely to suffer from heat on a trip, they often get a soaking bath before they go into the cars.

There is a rule that animals must not travel more than a day and a half cooped up in a car. So trains stop at resting pens along the way to let the animals out for exercise and food and water. After a few hours they are loaded again. Meantime the cars have had fresh clean sand or straw spread around on the floor. Some very fast stock trains zip along at such high speed that they reach the market before the animals need to stop and rest.

Veterinaries and inspectors often work at stock stations, looking out for animals that are sick. Caretakers for poultry and animals usually go along in the caboose.

## TANK CARS

Railroaders call a tank car a can. It really is an enormous can with different kinds of lining for hauling different liquids. Milk tanks have glass or steel linings. Tanks for certain chemicals are lined with rubber or aluminum or lead.

Altogether there are more than two hundred types of tank car, and here are some of the things that travel in them: fuel oil, gasoline, asphalt, molasses, syrup, turpentine, alcohol, cleaning fluid, lard, corn oil, and fish oil for vitamins.

Some tank cars have heating coils that warm up lard or molasses and keep it from getting too stiff to flow out easily. Most tank cars have a dome on top. If they didn't, they might burst open at the seams when the liquid inside them begins to expand in hot weather. Instead, the liquid bulges up into the dome, and no harm is done.

Wine tank cars have four compartments for carrying different kinds of wine.

Milk tank cars are built with two compartments that tip slightly toward the center so that every bit of milk will flow out. Each compartment is rather like a thermos bottle, with special wrapping around it to keep the milk from getting warm and sour. And the tanks are always filled brim full so the milk won't slosh around and churn up a batch of butter on the road. Can you guess why milk tanks don't need domes? Remember the milk must stay cool. Even when the sun is hot outside, the cool milk doesn't expand, so no dome is needed to keep the tank from bursting.

## HOPPERS AND GONDOLAS

A whole train made up of nothing but cars loaded with coal is called a black snake. Since rain and snow won't hurt coal, it travels in cars without tops. One kind of coal car has sloping ends like those on this page. It is called a hopper car. You load the coal in at the top, but you unload it by opening trapdoors in the bottom which let the coal drop into chutes.

Coal also travels in gondolas, which are just square-ended bins on wheels. They have to be unloaded by hand or by a dumping machine. It is hard to believe how fast some of these machines work. First a switch engine pushes the car of coal onto a platform underneath a tower. Grippers hold the car tight while it is jerked up, tilted over on its side, dumped, then let down again empty. The whole job takes only a minute or a minute and a half. The empty car rolls away downhill while a full one is being switched into place.

Another kind of dumper, the one you see in the picture, looks rather like a barrel that can roll from side to side. It, too, tips the car, spills out the coal, then swings back and lets the car drift downhill.

Other things besides coal can travel in hoppers and gondolas: ore, lumber, chemicals. Sugar is often carried in covered hoppers. These have tight lids and special linings, and they are kept very clean.

PIGGYBACKS

Watch a freight train and you will probably see some flat cars that are carrying truck trailers — the very same trailers that also travel on highways. Railroad people call this piggybacking, because a small freight carrier is getting a ride on a big freight carrier. The trailers are loaded with cargo in one city. Then

they take a long piggyback ride to another city where truck drivers are waiting to drive them through the streets and deliver the cargo. Truck companies say that this way of delivering freight saves money because one engine hauls many trailers.

GRAIN CARS

Early every summer the railroads put a lot of boxcars in the bank. That means they switch the cars off onto sidings all through the wheat-growing part of the country. Then, when the wheat is harvested and ready to be shipped to market, the cars can be drawn out of the bank, filled up with grain, and hauled away.

The wheat gets ripe in the south first. When harvest is finished there, the cars move along. All through the summer the grain cars work their way farther north.

Special grain doors have to be fitted in tight, just behind the regular sliding doors of the boxcars, to keep the wheat from leaking out. The grain doors go almost all the way to the top, but not quite. In a minute you'll see why.

After the farmers thresh their wheat, they take it to an elevator, which is an enormous storage tower close to the railroad tracks. Then, a chute from the elevator loads the wheat into the cars through the space at the top of the grain doors.

When a car is loaded, a man crawls in on top of the grain and hunches himself along with elbows and toes. He is the grain sampler who works for the companies that buy the wheat. Every once in a while he pokes a gadget down into the grain and brings up a sample from various parts of the car. These samples are enough to tell him whether the whole car is fair, good, or excellent wheat.

There is only about a two-foot space between the top of the grain and the roof of the car. So grain samplers have to be skinny men who can creep about easily.

## ODD SHAPES AND SIZES

Besides the ordinary cars that do ordinary jobs, railroads have some cars that have been made for special purposes.

A medical car is really a small traveling hospital. It goes along with construction crews when they have a big job to do far from a station. A trained nurse has her office in the car. She can take care of small injuries or give first aid until a doctor arrives.

One special car looks like a load of big sausages. It is really a sort of boxcar frame into which long, heavy pipes have been fitted so that they wind back and forth. The pipes carry a load of helium gas. Helium is used in balloons and blimps, because it is very light and it can't catch fire. Even when this car is fully loaded with all the gas that can be squeezed into the pipes, it weighs only a ton more than an empty car. Most loaded freight cars weigh between forty and eighty tons.

Sometimes a factory wants to ship a very tall machine by freight. So the railroad has it loaded onto an underslung flat car that looks as if it had had a bite taken out of its middle. It's called a depressed center car.

But still the machine may stick up too high to go through underpasses. Then a special department gets to work figuring out what to do. Men who know every mile of track work out a route that has no low underpasses. This sometimes means that the machine will make a dozen detours before it is delivered.

Circus cars are sometimes just flat cars which carry the animals' cages. But some of them are specially built

like stables, with stalls and a storage place for food. Fancy race horses ride in padded stable cars, too.

A pickle car is made of six separate wooden tanks. Men at the pickle works fill them with cucumbers and brine. Then the car delivers them at the factory to be bottled.

## TRESTLES, TUNNELS AND THINGS

Have you ever wondered why some railroad bridges across rivers are so very high, while automobile bridges are quite low? The trains look a little scary, rushing along way up in the air. But there's a good reason why they do it, and those tall trestles are so wonderfully planned and built that they are very safe.

Trains can't climb hills nearly as well as automobiles can. The slopes that trains go up must be very gentle ones. Even a very little bit of up-grade can slow a train a great deal. So the men who build railroads try to make the tracks run along as nearly level as possible. Next time you see a high bridge across a river, look at the rest of the country around. You'll see that the river cuts deep down between two hills. The bridge is built on tall stilts that make a level path for the train from one hillside to the other.

When trains have to go up or down a very long hill, the builders have a problem. They must slope the

tracks very gradually. In mountains this means that the tracks zig-zag back and forth, with long, wide curves between the zigs and the zags. If you look back at the picture on page 19, you will see how one railroad solved the problem. The rails are laid so that they spiral upward, making a loop. When a very long train travels along the loop, it's like a huge snake coiled around over its own tail!

Unless it's absolutely necessary, the builders try not to make curves. Trains run faster along rails that are straight as well as flat. Every bend means that the engineer has to slow down a little.

And so there are two reasons why railroads often have tunnels right through mountains. Instead of climbing far up and then coming down in long, slow curves, the train can run quickly straight through.

Tunnels are hard to dig. They often have to be blasted out of solid rock. So the builders don't make them any bigger than they have to. Of course, there's not room for a man to stand up on top of a freight car as it goes through a tunnel. To protect brakemen who might forget, there is a device called a tell-tale close to the mouth of a tunnel. It is simply a fringe of cords hanging down from a tall bar across the track. The cords touch the careless brakeman and warn him to get down right away before he's scraped off and hurt.

If you started in the morning, it would take you till night just to name the inventions that have made railroading more safe than it was a hundred years ago. Some of them are simple things like a tell-tale. Others, such as air brakes, are complicated. The most wonderful invention of all took hundreds of scientists a long

time to work out. It's called Centralized Traffic Control, or CTC.

To see what CTC does, you'll first have to imagine a stretch of railroad way out in the country, thirty miles from any station. There's just one main track, with sidings where trains running in opposite directions can pass each other. Each engineer has his train orders, so he knows whether he's supposed to go onto the siding or continue straight through. But unexpected things can always happen. If a train is late, it may not get to the siding on time. Then there will be danger of a collision.

That's where CTC comes in. Trains cannot bump into each other when CTC is at work. It is a wonderful system of electric wires that run along the tracks, all the way to an office building in a railroad town. The wires end in a long board that's dotted with lights and small levers. Now when train wheels travel over the rails, the wires carry electric messages to  that long board. Lights flash on and tell the man who watches the board exactly where the train is. If he wants it to go onto a siding, he pushes a lever. Electric switches miles away guide the train's wheels off the main track. At the same time, signal lights along the track tell the engineer to stop. Another set of lights inside the cab can also flash signals to the engineer.

The CTC has its own safety devices built into the switches. It will not let the man at the board make a mistake. He cannot push levers that might allow two trains to bump into each other.

In the old days, trains that ran through western ranch country were often late. The crew who had or-

ders to pull onto a siding knew they might have to wait
a long time. So they could just take a walk to the nearest house, wake the rancher and settle down for a visit.
If their host was in a good humor, he'd build a fire and
cook them a meal. Then, when they heard the whistle
of the approaching train, they'd start back in plenty of
time to signal as it passed their siding. Railroaders have
fun talking about those early times, but they'd really
rather have the safety of Centralized Traffic Control.

CTC helps to keep passenger trains moving safely
into big cities, too. The man at the board — he's called
the dispatcher — decides which track each train should
use. He pushes the levers. Electric switches move. Signals flash to the engineer, and lights on the board show
every train moving along.

## THE CAPTAIN AND THE CARS

The conductor of a passenger train is the man who takes tickets and says "All Aboard." But he does much more than that. He gets the train orders and makes sure that the other men in the crew understand them. He sees that the whole train is inspected while it is running, and if anything goes wrong, he gets it fixed. He is in charge of everything. Even the engineer must follow his signals. That is why they call the conductor the Captain.

The brakeman is the conductor's helper. He takes tickets. He checks the warning lights at the back of the train. He tests the brakes. When the train stops at a station he almost always walks up and down the platform. But he is not just stretching his legs. He is making a walking inspection to be sure that the cars are in good order.

On the fast streamlined trains, the conductor has a great deal of work to do. Many of the passengers are making long trips, so they have complicated tickets that allow them to stop at several places and then come home again. The conductor has to check the tickets and make sure they are right.

On short trips, conductors and brakemen take care of everything. But on long trips a streamliner needs other people who do special jobs. One of them is the stewardess. She makes passengers comfortable. She answers questions. At night she brings pillows to coach passengers. In some cars, each seat has a leg-rest that she pulls out, making a sort of couch for anyone who wants a nap.

If there are small babies on the train, the stewardess takes care of their bottles. On trains that have a special playroom for children, she reads stories or plays records.

A streamliner is really a sort of hotel on wheels. The observation car has big soft chairs and sofas, tables full of magazines, a radio, and desks for writing letters. At one end is a telephone booth where you can make calls to people just the way you do at home. This telephone works by radio. The radio operator on the train connects you with a regular telephone operator who completes the call over ordinary phone wires.

A few very, very fancy trains have a barbershop and a place where you can get your clothes pressed and your shoes shined.

Most fun of all are the streamliners with double-

decker cars called dome cars. The top deck is covered with a dome that looks something like an extra-large cupola on a caboose. Like the freight brakeman, you can sit and look out through the windows in the dome and see everything around you. In some dome cars there are tables where you can have something to eat.

Streamliners go very fast, but not too fast for safety. Beside the track are signs that tell the engineer what the speed limits are, and he pays attention to them. A powerful headlamp on the locomotive lights the track at night. Some trains have a bright, moving light in the rear, too. It flashes a figure-eight-shaped beam across the sky when the train is stopped and warns all others not to bump into it from behind.

## THE DINING CAR

The galley is the kitchen in the dining car. When you see all the food that has to be loaded into the diner for one trip, you can't believe there's any space left for cooking. But everything has been planned ahead of time so that it all fits.

The cooks and waiters have been to a school where they learned how to prepare and serve food for dozens of people without cluttering up the galley or getting in each other's way. The head cook is called the chef. He roasts the meat and carves it and decorates the fancy plates of food. The second cook fries and broils meat and bakes hot bread. The third cook cooks the vegetables and soup and coffee. The fourth cook peels vegetables and washes the dishes.

69

People eat so much on diners that railroads buy bananas by the boatload, meat and butter and coffee by the carload. One road has its own potato farm and turkey ranch.

A table for two people in a diner is called a deuce. One for four people is a large. When a waiter has customers sitting at all his tables, he says that he is flattened out. And if he makes a mistake or gets nervous, the others say he has gone up a tree.

It is fun to eat on a train, but the railroads themselves are very serious about food. They have experts who plan special menus to please boys and girls. They figure out new ways of serving food so that it looks and tastes like Thanksgiving all year round. One road even asked scientists to grow fancy roses for the dining tables and to invent a chemical that could be mixed with water to keep the roses fresh!

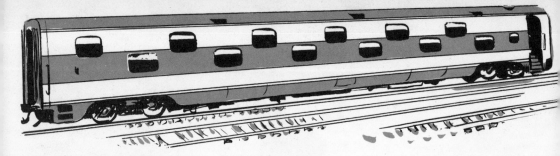

## SLEEPING

Some sleeping cars are called Pullman cars because the company that makes them was started by a man named Pullman. He built the first real sleeping cars about a hundred years ago. He also built some that he called hotel cars because people could sleep in one end and eat in the other end.

For a long time most sleepers had two rows of double seats with an aisle down the middle of the car. At night the porter made each pair of seats into a lower berth and pulled an upper berth down from its storage place in the wall. Then he hung green curtains from the ceiling to the floor all along the aisle.

People who slept in upper berths climbed up and down a ladder. A button in each berth flashed a light

THIS COMFORTABLE CHAIR SEAT IN THE DAYTIME...

BECOMES A SOFT BED AT NIGHT

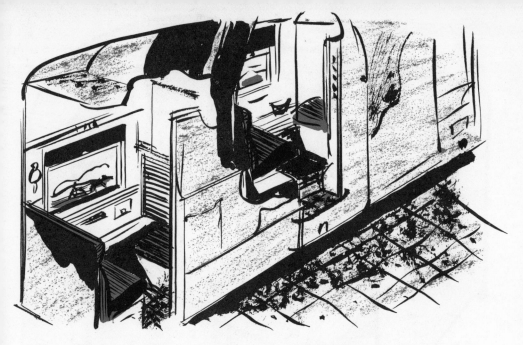

to call the porter. A little hammock hung against the wall. In it you put your clothes and small packages. At the ends of the car were dressing rooms and toilets.

The railroads still have a few of these Pullman cars. It is still fun to ride in them. But most sleeping cars are now made with lots of little separate rooms. One kind of car is called a duplex. It has checkerboard windows outside. Inside are small rooms, some on the lower level, some on the top level, with stairs leading to a corridor along the side. The rooms have sofa seats for daytime. At night, when you pull a handle in the wall, out slides a bed all made up and ready to be slept in.

Another kind of sleeping car has a row of small rooms

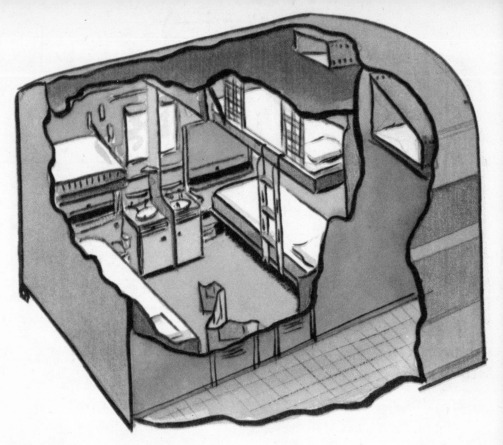

called roomettes all on one level. Each one of them
has its folding bed. There's also a washbowl, toilet and
clothes closet. An air-conditioner switch will make the
room warmer or cooler, and you can even turn on a
radio.

Other kinds of sleeping-car rooms have beds for two
or three people. Some are called drawing rooms. Others
are called compartments. They have arm chairs that
fold up at night. Connecting double bedrooms can be
turned into a travelling home for a family.

## SPECIAL TRAINS

Snow trains carry people who want to go skiing. They leave early Sunday morning, wait all day on a siding at a station near a good skiing place, and come back in the evening.

You can't always be sure ahead of time exactly where the train will stop. The snow may melt fast on one mountainside, so the railroad has to send the snow train to another place where the skiing is still good.

A snow train has a baggage car that is fixed up like a store where you can buy or rent any kind of skiing equipment. It has a diner where you eat your break-

fast, lunch and dinner or have a hot snack when you get cold.

For long trips to deep-snow country, you start Saturday night in a sleeping car and get back early Monday morning.

AT THE HEAD END

At the head end, a streamlined train has several cars that are different from passenger cars. One of them is built for the people who work on the train. It has berths where they sleep, shower rooms, lockers for clothes. The conductor may have an office there, and so may the man who is in charge of the dining car. (The men in the engine crew, of course, don't stay with the train. They change at division points.)

Some trains take a Railway Post Office car along at the head end. It does the work of a small post office. Regular mail clerks in the car sort letters and cancel the stamps and make bundles of all the postcards and letters that are supposed to go to the same place.

At stations where the train doesn't stop, the clerks toss bags of mail out onto the platform. At the same time a long metal arm attached to the car reaches out and picks up mailbags that hang from cranes beside the track. The mail in the bags is sorted right away.

The men who work in the Post Office car have

learned to be very accurate and fast. They need to know the names and locations of hundreds of towns and cities, so they can toss each letter into exactly the right sorting bag.

The Railway Express car carries packages of all kinds. It has refrigerated boxes for small quantities of things like fresh flowers and fish.

The idea for express cars started long ago, before the government's regular post office system had been worked out well. In those days, people often wanted to send valuable packages or letters in a hurry, but they had no way to do it. So some young men, who were known to be very honest, took on the job. Sometimes they carried parcels or letters in locked bags — sometimes in their own tall stovepipe hats! Gradually

they got so much business that they had to hire a whole car from the railroad. They were the grandfathers of the Railway Express that now owns hundreds of cars.

In springtime, the express man often travels with noisy cargo. That is the season when chicken farmers begin sending baby chicks in boxes all over the country.

Pet animals usually ride in the baggage car, along with suitcases, trunks and bicycles. All kinds of pets travel on trains. You check them, just the way you check a suitcase, and the baggageman takes care of

them. He is used to dogs and cats and birds, but once a baggageman had to mind a huge sea cow all the way from New York to St. Louis.

Sometimes dogs get so fond of trains that they spend their whole lives riding with friendly engineers or baggagemen. Cooks and waiters in the diner save scraps for them to eat.

The most famous traveller of all was a Scotch terrier named Owney. During his long life he covered more than 150,000 miles, riding in Railway Post Office cars. The men put tags on his collar showing where he had been. Finally he collected so many tags that he had to have a harness to hold them. When he died, the Post Office Department had him stuffed and put in its museum.

NARROW GAUGE TRAINS

When your great-grandmother was a girl, fast trains ran from coast to coast and slower ones climbed to towns high in the mountains. Super-highways for automobiles and trucks were something that only a few people even imagined then. So — if freight and passengers were going far, they usually travelled by train. Mountains gave the railroads a lot of trouble, because it was hard to dig wide roadbeds along the steep, rocky

hillsides or to push them through tunnels in solid stone.

One answer to the problem was to make the tracks not so wide and the tunnels not so high and the trains not so big! These railroads were called narrow gauge. (Gauge means the distance between the tracks.) The trains looked like toys, but they carried on their jobs perfectly well. A narrow-gauge engine and cars could whip easily around sharp curves, hugging the side of the cliff. The pint-sized locomotives pulled heavy loads. Elegant ladies and gentlemen used to travel in the tiny cars which were just as fancy as the big streamliners are now — maybe even fancier.

When good highways and huge trailer trucks came along, most of the narrow gauge railroads stopped run-

ning. A truck and trailer cost a lot less to operate than even a toy-like locomotive and freight cars. But in a few places you can still see the little giants at work. For instance, there is the Edaville Railroad which runs through the cranberry bogs in Massachusetts.

The narrow gauge Edaville trains haul boxes into the bogs where pickers fill them with berries. Then the loaded cars take the berries out to a cleaning and sorting shed for shipment to canneries and stores.

On many trips the Edaville trains carry passengers, too, for people love to ride behind the old-time engines. The man who owns the railroad lets everyone travel free, but if you want a souvenir ticket, you can buy it for a nickel!

BIG LIZ

## ALONG THE TRACKS

Section crews lay new railroad tracks and keep the old ones repaired. The men in each crew work on their own section of the road. They used to be called gandy dancers, and the boss of the crew was the king snipe. Nowadays some railroads don't have real sections. They just send track men to work wherever they happen to be needed.

In the old days repair work was done with hand tools. Men lifted the heavy rails with tongs. They chipped out the notches in the wooden ties for the rails to rest in. They hammered down the spikes that held the rails. They rode to work on a handcar, pumping a lever up and down to make the wheels turn.

Now there are motor cars instead of handcars, and

wonderful machines help with the work. A rail-laying crane lifts the rails and swings them into place on the ties. An adzer with whirling knife-blades cuts the notches. The spikes still have to be started into their holes by hand, but a mechanical hammer that runs by compressed air finishes the pounding job.

Perhaps you have noticed that railroad ties always rest in a bed of gravel or cinders or even squashed-up oyster shells. All these things are called ballast. When it rains or snows, the loose, pebbly ballast lets the water run off quickly, so that the ties will dry out and keep from rotting.

Weeds don't grow very well in ballast, but when they do a motor car comes along and kills them off with a chemical spray. Some railroads use a helicopter for spraying. When the ballast gets very dirty, a huge cleaning machine goes to work. The machine is called the Big Liz. It moves down the track, scooping up ballast and sifting out all

TRACK LAYER

the dust and junk. Then it squirts the cleaned ballast out again, leaving a clean roadbed behind.

Section crews often have portable telephones or walkie-talkies that save a lot of time. If they need materials, they call up the office and put in the order right away. And if the job takes longer than they expected, they phone a warning to the nearest station where trains can wait until it's safe to go ahead.

How does the section crew know when it is necessary to put in a new rail? In the old days the men got orders from an inspector who walked or rode slowly along in an inspection car, looking for cracks or breaks. Today there are machine-detectives that find cracks so small a man couldn't even see them.

The machine rides in a detector car, and it works by electricity, with tubes something like radio tubes.

The men who run it simply look at wavy lines drawn on paper by pens that are part of the machine. Whenever the car passes over a cracked rail, the pens make a very special kind of line. At the same time the machine automatically squirts out a little paint on the rail. Now the section crew can see where to put in a new one. Summer and winter, the detector cars creep along, making sure that the tracks are safe.

In winter, of course, the tracks must be kept clear. If there's just an ordinary snowfall, a powerful locomotive can run through it with no trouble. But when drifts get deep and heavy, the snow plow must go to work.

The man who first invented railroad snow plows got the idea from watching a windmill. He saw how the windmill blades tossed snow around as it fell. Why couldn't blades at the front of an engine cut into drifts and toss the snow off to one side? Of course they could. Railroads began using powerful rotary plows. The whirling blades chew into the deepest drifts, break up the snow and blow it away to the side of the track.

TIE ADZER

## OLD-TIME TRAVEL

The very first passenger cars were really stage-coaches with railroad wheels, and that's why we still use the name coach. Some old-time passenger cars had two decks. All the cars were fastened together with chains, so they bumped and banged each other when the train started or stopped. Sparks from the woodburning loco-motive flew back and set clothes on fire. Rails were only thin strips of iron nailed to wood. Sometimes the strips broke loose and jabbed right up through a car.

In the beginning, an engine had no closed-in cab for the engineer and fireman. They didn't want to be closed in. It was safer to stand outside so they could jump off quickly in case of accident. Cows on the track often caused trouble. Then a man named Isaac Dripps in-vented a cowcatcher made of sharp spears. But farmers complained that it killed too many animals, so scoop-shaped cowcatchers were installed. The name for a cowcatcher now is pilot.

The first headlight was a wood fire built on a small flat car pushed ahead of the engine. Later, whale-oil and kerosene lamps showed the way at night.

Engineers were once allowed to invent and tinker with their own whistles, and they worked out fancy ways of blowing them. This was called quilling. People along the tracks could tell who the engineer was by listening to the sound of his whistle. Some great quillers could even blow a sort of tune.

One engineer fixed his whistle so that people thought it was magic. Every time he blew it, the kerosene lights in the station went out! What happened was this: The whistle made vibrations in the air that were just right for putting out the lamps. But they did the same thing to signal lights, and so the engineer had to change his tune.

The first sleeping cars had rows of hard double-decker and even triple-decker bunks, with a stove at each end. Passengers brought their own blankets and pillows, and their own candles to see by. Nobody really slept much.

Trains were uncomfortable — even dangerous. But people needed them, and they were excited about them, too. All over the country men built new railroads as fast as they could. Each new company built as it pleased, and trains owned by one company didn't run over another's tracks. Of course, that meant you had to change trains often — wherever one railroad line stopped and another began. There were no railroad bridges over rivers, either. So you got off and took a ferry across.

One by one, men made inventions for trains, so that traveling became safer and more comfortable. En-

gines began to burn coal instead of wood. A piece of wire screen in the smokestack stopped the flying sparks. Coaches and sleepers had radiators that were warmed by hot water from the engine. They had softer seats, too. But they were still noisy for a long time because they had wooden bodies that creaked while the wheels clattered along.

Thirsty travelers at first had to buy drinks from the water boy who walked back and forth through the train. Later, cars had a tank of water and one glass for everyone to use. The glass sat in a rack, and it had a round bottom so that it wouldn't be of much use to a passenger who was tempted to steal it.

Lots of things about trains were different in the old days, but one thing was the same. They were just as much fun to ride in then as they are now.

## RAILROADING TALK

Here are more of the slang words that railroaders have made up:

BALLING THE JACK — this is what they say when they mean a train is going very fast. Highballing means the same thing.

BEND THE IRON — the switchman says he bends the iron when he changes the position of a switch.

BOOMER — a railroad worker who moves from place to place without sticking very long at any one job. There are still a few boomers, but in the old days there were thousands.

BUCKLE THE BALONIES — this means fasten together the air brake hoses which run underneath all the cars.

CHASE THE RED — this is what the flagman says he does when he goes back with a red flag or lantern to protect a stalled train.

CRADLE — a gondola or hopper car.

CUT — when a group of two or more freight cars are uncoupled from a train they are called a cut.

DOODLEBUG — a little railroad motor car that the section crew uses.

DOPE — the oily waste that is packed in journal boxes.

GARDEN — a freight yard.

GIVE HER THE GRIT — squirt sand onto a slippery track.

GREASE THE PIG — oil the engine.

HIGH IRON — the track that makes up the main line of a railroad, not switching track or station track.

RATTLER — a freight train.

SHOO-FLY — a track that is used only until regular track can be laid or repaired.

STRING OF VARNISH — a passenger train. High wheeler is another nickname.

# INDEX

Many railroading people helped to make this book. Here are some to whom the author and the artist want to give special thanks: Margaret Gossett; Inez M. DeVille of the Baltimore & Ohio Railroad; the late Lee Lyles of the Atchison, Topeka & Santa Fe Railway; C. J. Corliss and A. C. Browning of the Association of American Railroads; K. C. Ingram of the Southern Pacific Railroad; Eugene DuBois of the Pennsylvania Railroad; the staff in the President's office, Brotherhood of Railway Trainmen; Frank J. Newell of the Chicago, Milwaukee, St. Paul and Pacific Railroad; J. R. Sullivan of the New York Central Railroad; Howard A. Moulton of the New York, New Haven and Hartford Railroad; and finally to Harry Hall of the New York, New Haven and Hartford, through whose good offices the artist and his children spent a memorable day on the Edaville Railroad.

For help with the present revised edition, thanks go to Charles O. Morgret, George Martin and G. H. Newcomer of the Association of American Railroads; Milton Plumb of the Railway Labor Executives Association.